The Book o
Church J
A Collection of (Mostly) Clean Christian Chuckles

Compiled by Hugh Morrison

Montpelier Publishing
London
MMXV

ISBN-13:978-1507620632
ISBN-10:1507620632
Published by Montpelier Publishing, London.
Printed by Amazon Createspace.

A Sunday school teacher had told her class about Samson's riddle.

'Can anyone remember '"What is sweeter than honey, and what is stronger than a lion?"' she asked.

Little Johnny put up his hand. 'Tony the Tiger?'

*

Why should you always invite two Methodists to a dinner party?

Invite one, and he'll drink all your wine. Invite two, and they won't drink any.

*

'Are you a pillar of the church?'

'More of a flying buttress – I support it from the outside.'

*

New choirboy: 'if this is Evensong, is there going to be an Oddsong as well?'

Old choirboy: 'Just wait until the Vicar gets his guitar out.'

*

An elderly Anglican lady finally decided to read the Bible from cover to cover. When she'd finished, she spoke to the Rector after morning service. 'I really enjoyed reading the Bible,' she said, 'but I was surprised how much it quotes the Book of Common Prayer!'

Why are Anglicans such bad chess players?

Because they don't know the difference between a Bishop and a Queen.

*

'Who's that?' asked Little Johnny, pointing to a nun in church.

'A Sister of Charity,' replied his mother.

'Which one,' said Johnny. 'Faith or Hope?'

*

On the eve of the General Synod, a bishop was speaker at a prestigious dinner held in the City of London. He told a number of jokes which went down well with his audience, so he asked the journalists present to omit them from their reports, so that he could use them again in his speech at Synod the next day. Reporting on the dinner, one newspaper item stated 'The bishop told a number of stories that cannot be printed.'

*

Who was the greatest comedian in the Bible?

Samson. He brought the house down.

*

A clergyman named Canon Bull was preaching on Exodus Chapter 32, the making of the golden bull calf.

He asked the congregation, 'can anyone remember from the lesson what the Israelites made out of gold?'

There was silence so he gave them a hint. 'The clue is in my name.'

A voice piped up from the choir.

'Was it a cannon?'

*

Why was Pharaoh's daughter like a financier?

Because she drew a little prophet from the rushes on the banks.

*

A Sunday school teacher was talking to her class. 'We've learnt about all those kings and queens in the Bible, and about how powerful they were. But there is something higher, worth more than a king or queen. Can anyone tell me what it is?

Little Johnny put up his hand. 'Aces?'

*

How many charismatics does it take to change a lightbulb?

Two. One to change the bulb and the other to cast out the spirit of darkness.

*

A Victorian missionary was shipwrecked off the coast of Africa but managed to swim ashore. After walking for hours through the jungle he came across a hut. Terrified that it might be full of cannibals, he uttered a fervent prayer for deliverance. Suddenly he heard an angry shout from inside the hut.

'Deal the next card you swine, and pass that damned gin bottle!'

'Thank God,' cried the missionary. 'They're Christians!'

*

Why was the first day of Adam's life the longest?

Because it had no Eve.

*

'I very much enjoyed your sermon on the foolish virgins, vicar,' said young Miss Smith after the service. 'I intend never to be one again!'

*

An Anglican bishop prayed every day for Christian unity.

One day, God spoke to him. 'The good news is I have decided to answer your prayers,' boomed God from the heavens. 'From now on all Christians will be as one; there will be no more denominations nor schisms.'

The priest trembled with excitement.

'The bad news,' continued God, 'is that you're going to have to move to Rome.'

*

'Where two or three are gathered in my name'...that's usually Evensong.

*

Notice in church magazine: 'The preacher for next Sunday will be found pinned up in the church porch.'

It was the week before little Johnny's birthday, and he was on his knees at his bedside praying for presents in a very loud voice.

'Please send me,' he shouted, 'a bicycle, a cricket bat, a football…'

'What are you praying so loud for?' his younger brother interrupted. 'God isn't deaf.'

'I know he isn't,' said little Johnny, winking toward the next room, 'but granny is.'

*

What happened to the bellringer who got pulled up into the belfry?

He went like the clappers.

*

Little Johnny sat in church. The hymns were 'Jesus shall reign', 'Lo, He comes with clouds descending', 'Sun of my soul thou saviour dear' and finally 'All hail the power of Jesus' name'.

Confused, Johnny whispered to his mother, 'I wish Jesus would make his mind up about the weather.'

*

How many Anglicans does it take to change a lightbulb?

Over my dead body - my grandmother donated it!

*

A parish magazine interviewed a churchwarden who was retiring after 50 years' service.

'You must have seen a lot of changes in that time.'

'Yes,' came the reply. 'And I've resisted every single one of them.'

*

'What is the name of this boy,' asked the clergyman as his mother passed the baby to him.

'It's not a boy,' said the mother. 'Let go of my finger!'

*

A visitor to a small Welsh town which had four chapels, none of which were well attended, asked the minister of one dying congregation, 'How's your chapel getting on?' 'Not very well', he said, 'but, thank the Lord, the others are not doing any better.'

*

From a parish magazine: 'the new RAF memorial chapel will be dedicated to Douglas Bader, the wartime hero famous for being legless.'

*

Did you hear about the new liberal branch of the Church of England?

It has six commandments and four suggestions.

*

A Sunday school teacher asked, 'Why did David say he would rather be a door-keeper in the house of the Lord?'

6

'Because,' answered a boy, 'he could then walk outside while the sermon was being preached.'

*

Catholics don't recognise the Anglican communion.

Anglicans don't recognise the Pope.

Methodists don't recognise each other in the off-licence.

*

McTavish offered to collect money for the new church roof.

A week later, the minister met him in the street, staggering and reeling from side to side.

'How came you in this disgraceful condition, McTavish?' asked the minister, sternly.

'It was like this, minister,' he replied. 'Everyone I visited for money gave me a wee drop after making his donation.'

'Are there no teetotallers in this town?' asked the minister, shaking his head gravely.

'Oh aye,' replied McTavish, 'I've written to all of them.'

*

How do we know Samson was a cannibal?

Because he slaughtered the Philistines, and then went to Etam.

A bus driver and a priest from a mountainous village both died at the same time, and appeared before the Pearly Gates. St Peter allowed the bus driver in, but told the priest there was no vacancy.

The priest protested. 'But I'm a man of God – how can you keep me out and let that bus driver in? He was drunk half the time he drove round those mountain bends!'

'Well,' said St Peter, 'in your church everybody used to fall asleep. But as soon as they were in his bus, everybody used to start praying!'

*

If the tabloid press had existed in Biblical times, after Jesus walked on water the headlines would have read 'SON OF GOD CAN'T SWIM.'

*

How did Jonah feel when he was swallowed by the whale?

Down in the mouth.

*

A man wanted to become a bell-ringer, but he had no arms.

The vicar was concerned. 'How can you be a bell-ringer without arms?'

The man replied 'Arms? Who needs them!'

He then ran to the top of the bell tower, and started ringing the bell with his face. Unfortunately the effort required caused him to lose balance, and he fell from the bell tower into the church below.

The congregation gathered around him. The vicar said 'does anybody know his name?'

'I'm not sure,' said one of the congregation, 'but his face rings a bell.'

*

What was the first financial transaction in the Bible?

When Pharaoh received a check on the bank of the Red Sea, and Moses passed it.

*

A tourist from the American Bible Belt went to morning service at a Presbyterian church in the Western Isles of Scotland. It was soon evident that he was accustomed to a less formal atmosphere during worship, and from time to time interrupted the sermon and prayers by loudly exclaiming 'Praise the Lord!'

This went on for some time until an old Elder tapped the man on the shoulder and said sternly, 'We dinnae praise the Lord here!'

*

When did Adam and Eve cause an uproar?

When they raised Cain.

*

At a formal dinner, a businessman was boasting of his worldly success to a bishop. The bishop listened politely, then said:

'My good man, all this is most interesting – but I hope that you give thanks to your Creator for it.'

9

'I certainly do,' replied the businessman. 'I'm a self-made man!'

*

Why did the choirboy blush?

Because he looked at a rood screen.

*

A small boy pressed some coins into the minister's hand at the end of the service.

'What's this for, Johnny?' asked the minister, with a smile.

'I wanted to help you. My daddy said you're the poorest preacher we've ever had.'

*

What did Lot do when his wife turned to salt?

Got a fresh one.

*

How many Unitarians does it take to change a lightbulb?

We choose not to make a statement either in favour of or against the need for a light bulb. However, if in your own journey you have found that light bulbs work for you, you are invited to write a poem or compose a modern dance about your light bulb for the next Sunday service, in which we will explore a number of light bulb traditions, including incandescent, fluorescent, long-life and tinted, all of which are equally valid paths to luminescence.

What do you get if you cross a Unitarian with a Jehovah's Witness?

Someone who knocks on people's doors for no particular reason.

*

Why was Eve an ideal husband for Adam?

Because she was cut out for him.

*

An elderly bishop was walking along the cathedral close one day when he noticed a very small boy trying to press a doorbell on a house across the street. The boy was very small and the doorbell was too high for him to reach.

After watching the boy's efforts for some time, the cleric moved closer. He placed his hand kindly on the boy's shoulder, leant over and gave the doorbell a good ring.

Crouching down to the boy's level, the bishop smiled benevolently and asked, 'And now what do we do, young man?' To which the boy replied, 'Now we run!'

*

What is the first man mentioned in the Bible?

Chap. the first.

*

A story is told of the Duke of Wellington's new chaplain, who asked the great military man how long he might preach for.

'You may preach for as long as you wish,' said the Duke.

'Thank you indeed, my Lord,' said the clergyman, enthusiastically.

'...but I will listen for only 20 minutes,' added the Duke.

*

Who was the greatest financier in the Bible?

Noah; he was floating his stock while everyone was in liquidation.

*

An elderly and somewhat 'past it' vicar heard a popular preacher give a sermon on adultery to a packed church.

'The best years of my life were spent in the arms of another man's wife!' said the preacher. The congregation was shocked, until he added '...and that woman was my mother!' The congregation burst out laughing, and the sermon was a great success.

The next week, the vicar decided to use the line in his own church, but when he got to the pulpit, he couldn't quite recall how the joke went.

He announced loudly, 'the greatest years of my life were spent in the arms of another man's wife!' His parishioners recoiled in horror.

After standing there for almost a minute in the stunned silence, trying to recall the second half of the joke, the vicar finally blurted out, '...and I can't remember who she was!'

*

Where was Solomon's temple located?

On the side of his head.

From church magazine: Winners in the homemade wine section were Mrs Eltham (fruity, well-rounded), Mrs Tilling (fine colour and full-bodied), and Miss Ogilvy (slightly acid, but should improve if laid down).

*

What excuse did Adam give to his children as to why he no longer lived in Eden?

'Your mother ate us out of house and home.'

*

A country vicar became increasingly annoyed with the high prices charged in the village shop.

One day he reproved the shopkeeper by quoting the Scripture. 'The first shall be last and the last shall be first.'

'It makes no difference to me how you arrange 'em,' replied the tradesman. 'I'm just the middleman'.

*

Why was Moses the most sinful man in the Bible?

Because he broke all Ten Commandments at once.

*

From church magazine: 'the bishop spoke briefly, much to the delight of the audience.'

*

Why was Goliath surprised when David slew him with a pebble?

Because it had never entered his head before.

*

From a parish magazine: 'this month the Womens' Institute will be raising money by crocheting a new altar carpet. Anyone wanting to do something on the carpet should ask for a slip of paper.'

*

How many people left the Ark before Noah?

Three, because Noah went forth out of the Ark.

*

'I heard terrible language coming from your house this morning,' said the vicar to one of his parishioners.

'That was my wife, reverend,' replied the man. 'She couldn't find her prayer book.'

*

Why was Moses the best mathematician in the Bible?

Because he wrote the book of Numbers.

*

Vicar: 'The Bible tells us we should love our neighbours.'

Parishioner: 'Yes, but the Bible was written before our neighbours lived so close'.

Why was Samson the cheapest man to be enslaved?

Because Delilah got him for a snip.

*

Where is the first description of cannibalism in the Bible?

2 Kings 8:1

*

How do we know Noah had a pig in the ark?

Because he produced Ham.

*

Brother Benedict entered a monastery. The Abbott said, 'Brother, this is a silent order. You are welcome here as long as you wish, but you may not speak until I direct you to do so.'

Brother Benedict lived in the monastery for five years before the Abbott said to him: 'Brother Benedict, you have been here five years now. You may speak two words.'

Brother Benedict said, 'Hard Bed.'

'I'm sorry to hear that,' the Abbott said. 'We will get you a better bed.'

After another five years, Brother Benedict was called by the Abbott. 'You may say another two words, Brother Benedict.'

'Cold food,' said Brother Benedict. The Abbott promised him that the food would be better in the future.

On his fifteenth anniversary at the monastery, the Abbott again called Brother Benedict into his cell.

'Two words you may say today.'

'I resign,' said Brother Benedict.

'It is probably best,' sighed the Abbott. 'You've done nothing but complain since you got here.'

*

What did Luke have first and Paul have last?

The letter 'L'.

*

A prison chaplain was asked by some of the prisoners to pray for Annie Power. Willingly and gladly he did so for three Sundays in the prison chapel. On the fourth Sunday one of the felons told him he need not do it anymore.

'Why,' asked the good man, with an anxious look, 'is she dead?'

'Oh, no,' said the convict – 'she won the Grand National last week.'

*

Why didn't they play cards on the Ark?

Because Noah was standing on the deck.

*

Why did the Scotsman join the Free Church?

He thought it was the only one where you didn't have to pay anything.

*

What was it that Adam never possessed, but gave two of to his children?

Parents.

*

Little Johnny was at the kitchen table, carefully drawing a picture, his face fixed in concentration on the paper.

'What are you drawing, Johnny?' asked his mother.

'God,' said Little Johnny.

'But nobody knows what God looks like, Johnny,' chided his mother.

'They will when I've finished,' replied the boy.

*

At what time of day was Adam created?

A little before Eve.

*

'My sermon on austerity made a tremendous impression on the congregation.'

'How do you know?'

'I've just counted the collection.'

17

Why was Noah obliged to stoop on entering the ark?

Because, although the ark was high, Noah was a higher ark (hierarch).

*

Paddy went into the confession box.

'Bless me father, for I have sinned,' he said. 'I stole four thousand bricks, two tons of timber, five thousand roof tiles and twenty double glazed windows.'

'My son,' replied the priest, 'that is a terrible sin.'

'What should I do?' asked Paddy.

'My son, you will have to make a novena.'

'Sure and I don't know what that is,' replied Paddy, 'but if you've got the plans, I've got the materials.'

*

How long did Cain hate his brother?

As long as he was Abel.

*

A minister was sharing a rail compartment with a man the worse for drink, who insisted on talking.

'Please don't speak to me,' said the minister. 'You're drunk.'

'Drunk?' replied the man. 'You're worse than me — you've got your collar on back to front.'

Who was the fastest runner in the world?

Adam, because he was first in the race.

*

What three words did Adam use when he introduced himself to Eve which read backwards and forward the same?

Madam, I'm Adam.

*

Little Johnny attended his first Christmas service.

Afterwards he said to his mother, 'what's this "el" wot they haven't got?'

Confused, his mother asked 'what on earth do you mean?'

'They kept on singing "No-el, No-el"', said Little Johnny.

*

What is the difference between Noah's ark and Joan of Arc?

One was made of wood, the other was Maid of Orleans.

*

An Anglican priest was about to deliver his sermon. Approaching the microphone on the pulpit he tapped it and said: 'There's something wrong with this mike.' Immediately came the response: 'And also with you.'

Why didn't the Israelites starve in the desert?

Because of the sand which is there.

*

How came the sandwiches there?

Because Noah sent Ham, and his descendants mustered and bred.

*

Sunday school teacher: 'Who was responsible for the Writing on the Wall?'

Little Johnny: 'Please sir, it wasn't me!'

*

The secret of a good sermon is to have a good beginning and a good ending; and to have the two as close together as possible.

*

Little Johnny was in church at his first wedding. When it was over, he asked his mother, 'Why did the lady change her mind?'

'What do you mean?' asked his mother.

'Well,' replied Johnny, 'she went down the aisle with one man and came back with another.'

*

What are the three things a bride likes most in a church wedding service?

Aisle, altar, hymn. (I'll alter him).

*

During a terrible storm, a small ferry was sinking and the captain said to the passengers, 'is there anyone here who can pray?'

'I can,' said one of them, stepping forward. 'I am a minister of religion.'

'That's alright then,' said the captain. 'You start praying and the rest of us can put on lifejackets – we're one short.'

*

Why was Boaz unkind before he married?

Because he was Ruthless.

*

An old man went into the confession box.

'Father,' said the man, 'I am 80 years old. I have been married for 50 years. All these years I have been faithful to my wife, but yesterday I was intimate with a beautiful 18 year old girl.'

'When was the last time you made a confession?' asked the priest.

'I never have done, Father, I'm Jewish.'

'Then why are telling me all this?'

'I'm telling everybody!'

*

'Seamus, I hear you've been fighting', said Father O'Malley to his parishioner.

'Tis true I was, fathorr.'

'Don't you remember what the Bible says about turning the other cheek?'

'Yes fathorr, but the other feller hit me on the nose, and I've only got one o' them.'

*

The bishop died in the night, and the vicar gravely broke the news to his congregation in church the next morning.

'We will never see the bishop again. He has gone to heaven.'

*

Which man in the Bible had no father?

Joshua, the son of Nun.

*

Notice in church magazine: 'this Saturday the Womens' Guild will hold their annual jumble sale. Ladies, this is a good time to get rid of any unwanted items in your home. Don't forget to bring your husbands.'

*

Father O'Malley answered the phone.

'This is the tax office speaking. Do you know a Seamus O'Houlihan?'

'I do,' replied Father O'Malley.

'Is he a member of your congregation?'

'He is.'

'Did he donate five thousand Euros to the church?'

'He will,' said the priest.

*

'Will all denominations be welcome at the ecumenical service?'

'Of course! Particularly tens, twenties and fifties.'

*

It was Palm Sunday but because of a cold, Little Johnny had to stay at home with his mother while his father went to church. When his father returned home, he gave his son one of the palm fronds that had been handed out during the service.

'What's that for?' asked Little Johnny.

'People held them over Jesus' head as He walked by,' said his father.

'Typical,' said Little Johnny. 'The one Sunday I don't go, He shows up.'

*

Why was the whale who swallowed Jonah like the Perrier company?

Because he took a great prophet out of the water.

Two boys were walking home from Sunday school.

'What do you think about all this Satan stuff?' asked one.

'Well, remember what happened with Father Christmas,' said the other. 'It's probably just your dad.'

*

How does Moses make his coffee?

Hebrews it.

*

In old Ireland, Paddy went into the confession box.

'Father, I stole a chicken,' he whispered.

'That's a terrible sin, my son,' said the priest.

'Do you want it?' whispered Paddy.

'Certainly not,' replied the priest, shocked at the suggestion. 'Return it to the man you stole it from.'

'But I've tried, father, and he doesn't want it.'

'In that case, you may keep it yourself.'

Paddy went home with a clear conscience. The priest went home to find one of his chickens had been stolen.

A Scotsman was travelling by train seated next to a stern-faced clergyman. As the Scot pulled out a bottle of whisky from his pocket the clergyman glared and said reprovingly,

'Look here, I am sixty-five and I have never tasted whisky in my life!'

'Dinna worry, minister,' smiled the man, pouring himself a dram. 'There's no risk of you starting now!'

*

Notice in church magazine on a clergyman's recent illness: 'God is good: the vicar is better.'

*

In the deep south of the USA, a Baptist preacher was baptizing people in a river. A drunk staggered up to the preacher to see what was going on.

'Mister, are you ready to find Jesus?' asked the preacher.

'I sure am,' said the drunk. The preacher thrust the man's head under the water.

'Have you found Jesus yet?' asked the preacher after pulling him out.

'No sir,' said the drunk, so the preacher dunked him again.

The preacher pulled him out and said 'have you found Jesus yet?', louder this time.

'No sir I ain't,' said the drunk. 'Are you sure this is where he fell in?'

What kind of fur did Adam and Eve wear?

Bare skin.

*

A Catholic priest preached a fine sermon on married life and its beauties. Two old Irishwomen were heard coming out of church commenting on the address.

"Tis a fine sermon his Reverence would be after giving us,' said one to the other.

'It is, indade,' was the quick reply, 'and I wish I knew as little about the matter as he does.'

*

Why did Joseph's brothers throw him in the pit?

They thought it would be a good opening for him.

*

A young boy was visiting a church for the first time. He stopped at the war memorial. The boy asked the verger 'who are all those people?'

The verger replied, 'Those are the men of this parish who died in the services'.

Puzzled, the youngster asked, 'Was that the morning service or the evening service?

*

Where is the first mention of insurance in the Bible?

26

When Adam and Eve needed more coverage.

*

A drunk stumbled into church and sat in the confession box.

After a while, the priest became impatient and knocked on the panel.

There was no reply, and after a few minutes, the priest knocked more loudly.

'There's no use knocking,' slurred the drunk. 'There's no paper in this one either!'

*

From church magazine: 'Because of repair work by the west door, for the next few weeks we are going to christen babies at the other end. '

*

A small girl was asked why it was important to be quiet in church.

'So we don't wake anyone up' she replied.

*

'I'm 96 tomorrow, vicar, and I haven't an enemy in the world.'

'That is wonderful. You must truly have a forgiving nature.'

'No, I've just outlived them all!'

From a parish magazine: 'The Women's Guild is holding a jumble sale. Any woman with cast-off clothing should see the vicar after the service.'

*

Crossing a bridge, a Scots minister came across a man about to throw himself off.

'Stop, man!' cried the minister.

'Why should I?' wailed the man.

'There's so much to live for' said the minister. 'Are ye no a religious man?'

'Aye I am,' replied the suicidal one.

'A Christian?' asked the clergyman.

'I am that.'

'Protestant or Catholic?'

'Protestant' came the reply.

'Church of Scotland or Free Church?'

'Free Church, minister', said the man, beginning to relax a little.

'Reformed Free Church or Primitive Free Church?'

'Reformed Free Church,' said the man, thinking at last here was someone who understood him.

'Are ye of the original Reformed Free Church conventicle of 1849, or that of 1876?' asked the minister.

'Of 1876!' cried the suicidal one, offering to shake hands with the cleric.

'Go ahead and jump, ye damned heretic!' cried the minister.

*

Headline in a parish magazine: 'I upped my planned giving – up yours!'

*

In the Western Isles the minister met McTavish by the bus stop early on a Sunday morning.

With concern, he asked: 'Surely McTavish, you don't take the bus on the Sabbath day?'

'I'm sorry minister,' came the reply, 'but it's the only way I can get tae the harbour tae protest aboot the ferries runnin' on Sundays!'

*

From parish magazine: 'A talk will be held tonight on church security. You are invited to meet the parish councillors and beat officers.'

*

Who was the straightest man in the Bible?

Joseph, because the Pharaoh made him a ruler.

*

McNab was passing through a small highland town and knocked on the door of the manse.

'Minister, ye did me a favour ten years ago,' said McNab, 'and I have nivver forgotten it.'

'Ah,' replied the clergyman with a holy expression on his face, 'as the good book says, "there is more joy in heaven over one sinner that repenteth" – you've come back to repay me?'

'Not exactly,' replied McNab. 'I've just got into toon and need another favour, and I thought of you right away.'

*

Who is the smallest man in the Bible?

Peter, because he slept on his watch.

*

A good looking priest found the young ladies in the church rather too interested in him. At last it became so embarrassing that he left. Not long afterwards he met the priest who had succeeded him.

'Well,' he asked, 'how do you get on with the ladies?'

'Oh, very well indeed,' said the other. 'There is safety in numbers, you know.'

'Ah!' was the instant reply. 'I only found it in Exodus.'

*

Why didn't Noah go fishing?

He only had two worms.

The minister of a Methodist church noticed that old Tom, an impoverished pensioner, hadn't attended services for a couple of weeks. Concerned for the old man, the minister visited him at home and asked if he hadn't been to church because he'd been ill.

'It's not that, reverend' said the old man, who answered the door in his pyjamas. 'It's just that I tore me only suit, and I've nothing to go out in.'

The minister thought for a moment then remembered that someone had donated a beautiful tailored suit for the church jumble sale. He decided he would donate this to Tom, who accepted it later that day.

The next Sunday, Tom still didn't turn up for church. With growing concern, the minister visited him again.

'Wasn't the suit any good?' asked the clergyman.

'Oh there's nowt wrong with the suit, Reverend.'

'So why weren't you in church?'

'Oh I was, Reverend. The fact is, when I put that suit on, I looked so respectable I decided to join the Church of England.'

*

Note in parish magazine: 'the congregation is requested to stay seated until the end of the recession.'

*

Kelly's beloved dog died, so he put it in a box and went to his parish priest for a special mass to be said for the animal's soul.

'Look here, Kelly,' said the priest. 'Do ye not know that Catholic churches can't be after doing that sort of thing?'

Kelly looked crestfallen. Trying to be helpful, the priest said 'Why don't you take it to the protestant church down the road. They're after believing all kinds of things, and they might be able to do something for the poor creature.'

Kelly smiled. 'Aw thanks, father. That's grand. What do you think they'll charge me for the service? I'm willing to pay up to a thousand Euros.'

The priest suddenly put his arm around Kelly. 'Now why didn't you tell me the dog was Catholic?'

*

'I understand your vicar has gone to the Holy Land for a month.'

'Yes, that's right.'

'For a holiday, I suppose?'

'Yes, the bishop decided that we were entitled to one.'

*

Who was the smartest man in the Bible?

Abraham. He knew a Lot.

*

A Sunday-school teacher had been telling her class of little children about crowns of glory and heavenly rewards for good people.

'Now, tell me,' she said, at the close of the lesson, 'who will get the biggest crown?'

There was silence for a minute or two, then a bright little chap piped up: 'Him wot's got the biggest 'ead.'

*

A prominent atheist academic was the guest of honour at an Oxford college dinner. Just before the meal commenced, the Dean leant over to him and explained that it was strict college tradition to say Grace before eating.

Since the chaplain was off sick, it was also college tradition that the duty should then fall to the principal speaker. Not wishing to be rude, but acutely aware of his reputation, the academic rose to his feet and solemnly declared:

'There being no clergyman present, let us thank God.'

*

A stern priest in old Ireland had issued to his people a command against dancing, believing it to be a device of the devil. A few of the young people disobeyed and attended a dance given at a neighbouring town. Finally it reached the ears of the priest, and, meeting one of the culprits on the street one morning, he said in a stern voice:

'Good morning, child of the devil!'

'Good morning, father!' smilingly answered the girl.

*

A Methodist minister was invited to one of the royal chapels to preach.

'Do you require a surplice?' asked the chaplain.

'I am a Methodist. What do I know about surplices? All I know about is a deficit!'

*

The clergyman's eloquence may have been at fault, still he felt annoyed to find that an old gentleman fell asleep during the sermon on two consecutive Sundays. So, after service on the second week, he told the boy who accompanied the sleeper that he wished to speak to him in the vestry.

'Johnny, who is that elderly gentleman you attend church with?'

'Grandpa,' was the reply.

'Well,' said the clergyman, 'if you will keep him awake during my sermon, I'll give you fifty pence each week.'

The boy fell in with the arrangement, and for the next two weeks the old gentleman listened attentively to the sermon.

The third week, however, found him soundly asleep.

The vexed clergyman sent for the boy and said: 'I am very angry with you. Your grandpa was asleep again today. Didn't I promise you fifty pence a week to keep him awake?'

'Yes,' replied little Johnny, 'but grandpa now gives me a pound not to disturb him.'

*

An Irishman and a Jew were arguing. Finally the subject came round to their respective religions.

'I bet my priest knows more than your Rabbi,' the Irishman insisted.

'Of course he does' replied the Jew. 'You tell him everything.'

*

'Father,' said the minister's son, 'my teacher says that 'collect' and 'congregate' mean the same thing. Do they?'

'Perhaps they do, my son.' said the venerable clergyman; 'but you may tell your teacher that there is a vast difference between a congregation and a collection.'

*

Three clerics were discussing the problem of bats in their respective churches.

'We tried to establish a bat sanctuary in the church grounds, but they wouldn't move there,' said the Methodist minister.

'We sprinkled holy water all over their nesting places, but it attracted more of them than ever,' said the Catholic priest.

'Ah,' smiled the Anglican vicar. 'We got rid of them easily. We just baptised them all, and we haven't seen any of them since.'

*

Minister: 'You should be careful! Don't you know that drink is mankind's worst enemy?'

McTavish: 'Yes; but aren't we supposed tae love our enemies?'

*

Where is the first tennis match mentioned in the Bible?

When Joseph served in Pharaoh's court.

*

The chapel of a well known university has had to abandon its nativity play this year due to casting problems. They couldn't find three wise men or a virgin.

*

How many Presbyterians does it take to change a lightbulb?

100. One to change the lightbulb, and the other 99 to walk out in disgust about changes to the kirk.

*

Instead of his usual donation of a penny, McTavish accidentally put a ten pence piece in the collection plate at the kirk one Sunday.

The steward noticed the mistake, and in silence he passed by McTavish without offering the plate to him for nine more Sundays.

On the tenth Sunday, McTavish ignored the plate as usual, but the steward this time announced in a loud voice:

'Yer time's up, McTavish.'

*

A vicar told his congregation, 'Next week I plan to preach about the sin of lying. To help you understand my sermon, I want you all to read St Mark chapter 17.'

The following Sunday, as he prepared to deliver his sermon, the minister asked for a show of hands. He asked how many had read St Mark chapter 17. Every hand went up. The vicar smiled and said,

'The gospel of St Mark has only sixteen chapters. I will now proceed with my sermon on the sin of lying.'

*

Two Irish labourers were mending a road in Dublin, outside a 'house of ill repute'.

One day they saw an Anglican bishop enter the house.

'Tis terrible!' said Seamus. 'These protestants, visiting such a place!' The next day they observed a rabbi go into the establishment.

'A dreadful thing,' said Paddy. 'claiming to be a man of God and going to a house like that.'

The next day they noticed a Catholic priest entering the building. Paddy immediately took off his cap. 'Oh no, Seamus, look – one of the poor girls must have died.'

*

Where is mathematics first mentioned in the Bible?

When God told Adam and Eve to go forth and multiply.

*

A newly appointed Scots minister on his first Sunday of office had reason to complain of the poorness of the collection.

'Mon,' replied one of the elders, 'they are close, verra close.'

'But,' confidentially, 'the auld meenister he put three or four pennies intae the plate hissel', just to gie them a start. Of course he took the pennies awa' with him afterward.'

The new minister tried the same plan, but the next Sunday he again had to report a dismal failure. The total collection was not only small, but he was grieved to find that his own pennies were missing.

'Ye may be a better preacher than the auld meenister,' exclaimed the elder, 'but if ye had half the knowledge o' the world, an' o' yer ain flock in particular, ye'd ha' done what he did an' glued the pennies tae the plate.'

*

A minister was testing the children in his church to see if they understood the concept of getting to heaven. He asked them, 'If I sold my house and my car, had a big jumble sale and gave all my money to the church, would that get me into heaven?'

'NO!' the children answered.

'If I cleaned the church every day, looked after the grounds, and repainted the walls, would that get me into heaven?'

Again, the answer was 'No!'

'Well, then, persisted the minister, 'if I was kind to animals and gave sweeties to all the children, and loved my family, would that get me into heaven?'

Again, they all answered 'No!'

The clergyman continued, 'Then how CAN I get into heaven?'

A six year-old boy shouted out – 'You've got to be dead first!'

*

Seamus left the pub the worse for wear.He sat down on a bus next to a priest. His tie was stained, his face was plastered with red lipstick, and a half empty bottle of whisky was sticking out of his torn coat pocket. He opened a newspaper and began reading. Then he asked the priest,

'Father, what causes arthritis?'

'Well my son, it's the result of loose living, being with cheap, wicked women, too much whisky and a contempt for your fellow man.'

'Well I'll be damned!' Seamus muttered, returning to his paper.

The priest, feeling a little guilty, said, 'I'm very sorry. I didn't mean to upset you. How long have you had arthritis?'

'I don't, Father. But I was just reading here that the Pope does.'

*

Notice in a highland kirk magazine: 'If members of the congregation must put buttons in the collection, please provide your own buttons. Stop pulling them off the seat cushions.'

*

Notice in church magazine: 'the Young Mother's group will meet this Thursday. Anyone wishing to become a Young Mother should see the vicar after morning service.'

*

'I was pleased to see you at the kirk on Sunday, Jamesie,' said the minister.

'Och is that where I was?' replied Jamesie. 'I couldn't remember where on earth I went to after I left the pub.'

Notice in church magazine: 'Due to the Rector's illness, this Sunday's healing service is postponed until further notice.'

*

A Scots minister was speaking to his wife after service on Sunday night.

'The service went well,' observed his wife.

'Aye, good attendance - and a tourist was present, but I did not see him.'

'But how do you know? '

'There was a five pound note in the collection box.'

*

Item in church magazine: 'Last Saturday's recital was a great success. Thanks go to Mrs Frobisher for duty at the piano, which as usual fell on her.'

*

In rural Ireland, Seamus turned up for mass still the worse for wear after a night on the booze. He collapsed into a pew and fell asleep, snoring loudly.

The priest watched him from the pulpit with disgust, and decided to make an example of him.

He said to the congregation, 'All those wishing to have a place in heaven, please stand.'

The whole congregation stood except, of course, for Seamus, who was still fast asleep.

Then the priest said even more loudly, 'And he who would like to find a place in hell please STAND UP!'

Seamus, catching only the last part, groggily stood up, only to find that he was the only one standing.

Confused and embarrassed he said 'I don't know what we're voting on, Father, but sure, it seems like you and me are the only ones standin' for it!'

*

Notice in church magazine: 'A new loudspeaker system has been installed in the church. It was given by Mr Jones in memory of his wife.'

*

Two bishops were discussing the decline in morals in the modern world.

'I didn't sleep with my wife before I was married,' said one clergyman self-righteously, 'Did you?'

'I don't know,' said the other. 'What was her maiden name?'

Other books from Montpelier Publishing

Available from Amazon

Non-Corny Knock Knock Jokes: 150 super funny jokes for kids

A Little Book of Limericks: funny rhymes for all the family

A Little Book of Ripping Riddles and Confounding Conundrums

More Ripping Riddles and Confounding Conundrums

Riddles in Rhyme

A Little Book of Parlour Puzzles

The Bumper Book of Riddles, Puzzles and Rhymes

After Dinner Laughs: jokes and funny stories for speech makers

After Dinner Laughs 2: more jokes and funny stories for speech makers

Scottish Jokes: a Wee Book of Clean Caledonian Chuckles

Wedding Jokes: Hilarious Gags for your Best Man's Speech

Printed in Great Britain
by Amazon